# JAMES

## Put Your
## *Faith to Work*

*A Guided Discovery for Groups and Individuals*

**Kevin Perrotta**

LOYOLAPRESS.

CHICAGO

# LoyolaPress.

3441 N. Ashland Avenue
Chicago, Illinois 60657

*Nihil Obstat*
Reverend John Lodge, S.T.D.
Censor Deputatus
December 11, 2001

*Imprimatur*
Most Reverend Raymond E. Goedert, M.A., S.T.L., J.C.L.
Vicar General
Archdiocese of Chicago
December 11, 2001

The *Nihil Obstat* and *Imprimatur* are official declarations that a book is free of doctrinal and moral error. No implication is contained therein that those who have granted the *Nihil Obstat* and *Imprimatur* agree with the content, opinions, or statements expressed.

The Scripture quotations contained herein are from the New Revised Standard Version Bible: Catholic Edition, copyright © 1993 and 1989 by the Division of Christian Education of the National Council of the Churches of Christ in the U.S.A. Used by permission. All rights reserved. Subheadings in Scripture quotations have been added by Kevin Perrotta.

The Latin text of Bede's commentary on James (p. 21) can be found in *Corpus Christianorum Series Latina*, vol. 121 (Turnhout, Belgium: Typographi Brepols, 1983). Translation by Kevin Perrotta. An English translation is available in David Hurst, O.S.B., trans., *The Commentary on the Seven Catholic Epistles of Bede the Venerable* (Kalamazoo, Mich.: Cistercian Publications, 1985).

An English translation of Søren Kierkegaard's essay, "What Is Required to Look at Oneself with True Blessing in the Mirror of the Word?" (p. 31) can be found in Søren Kierkegaard, *For Self-Examination; Judge for Yourself!* Howard V. Hong and Edna H. Hong, eds. and trans. (Princeton, N.J.: Princeton University Press, 1990).

The Sigrid Undset quotations (p. 51) are from *Stages on the Road*, Arthur G. Chater, trans. (New York: Alfred A. Knopf, 1934), 209–22.

The Latin text of St. Francis's prayer (p. 60) can be found in *B.P. Francisci Assiatis Opuscula* (Antwerp: Officina Plantiniana Balthasaris Moreti, 1623), 97–98. Translation by Kevin Perrotta. An English translation is available in Regis J. Armstrong, O.F.M. Cap., and Ignatius C. Brady, O.F.M., trans., *Praying with Saint Francis* (Grand Rapids, Mich.: W. B. Eerdmans, 1996), 19–23.

The Latin text of Robert Bellarmine's *The Sighing of the Dove, Or the Value of Tears* (De gemitu columbae) (p. 61) can be found in Roberto Bellarmini Politiani, S.J., *Opera omnia*, vol. 8 (Naples: C. Pedone Lauriel, 1872). Translation by Kevin Perrotta.

*Interior design by Kay Hartmann/Communique Design*
*Illustration by Charise Mericle Harper*

ISBN 0-8294-1811-3

Printed in the United States of America
07 08 09 10 Bang 10 9 8 7 6 5

# Contents

## How to Use This Guide

You might compare the Bible to a national park. The park is so large that you could spend months, even years, getting to know it. But a brief visit, if carefully planned, can be enjoyable and worthwhile. In a few hours you can drive through the park and pull over at a handful of sites. At each stop you can get out of the car, take a short trail through the woods, listen to the wind blowing through the trees, get a feel for the place.

In this booklet we'll travel through a small portion of the Bible—the letter of James. Because the letter is short, we will be able to take a leisurely walk through it, thinking carefully about what we are reading and what it means for our lives today. Despite its brevity, the letter gives us a great deal to reflect on, for James deals with basic issues regarding our response to God's love.

This guide provides everything you need to begin exploring James in six discussions—or to do a six-part exploration on your own. The introduction on page 6 will prepare you to get the most out of your reading. The weekly sections provide explanations that highlight what James's words mean for us today. Equally important, each section supplies questions that will launch your group into fruitful discussion, helping you to both explore the letter for yourself and learn from one another. If you're using the booklet by yourself, the questions will spur your personal reflection.

Each discussion is meant to be a *guided discovery.*

**Guided.** None of us is equipped to read the Bible without help. We read the Bible *for* ourselves but not *by* ourselves. Scripture was written to be understood and applied in the community of faith. So each week "A Guide to the Reading," drawing on the work of both modern biblical scholars and Christian writers of the past, supplies background and explanations. The guide will help you grasp James's message. Think of it as a friendly park ranger who points out noteworthy details and explains what you're looking at so you can appreciate things for yourself.

**Discovery.** The purpose is for *you* to interact with this New Testament letter. "Questions for Careful Reading" is a tool to help you dig into the text and examine it carefully. "Questions for Application" will help you consider what James's words mean for your life here and now. Each week concludes with an "Approach to Prayer" section that helps you respond to God's word. Supplementary "Living Tradition" and "Saints in the Making" sections offer the thoughts and experiences of Christians past and present in order to show you what the letter of James has meant to others—so that you can consider what it might mean for you.

**How long are the discussion sessions?** We've assumed you will have about an hour and a half when you get together. If you have less time, you'll find that most of the elements can be shortened somewhat.

**Is homework necessary?** You will get the most out of your discussions if you read the weekly material and prepare your answers to the questions in advance of each meeting. But if participants are not able to prepare, have someone read the "Guide to the Reading" sections aloud to the group at the points where they occur in the weekly material.

**What about leadership?** If you happen to have a world-class biblical scholar in your group, by all means ask him or her to lead the discussions. But in the absence of any professional Scripture scholars, or even accomplished amateur biblical scholars, you can still have a first-class Bible discussion. Choose two or three people to take turns as facilitators and have everyone read "Suggestions for Bible Discussion Groups" (page 76) before beginning.

**Does everyone need a guide? a Bible?** Everyone in the group will need their own copy of this booklet. It contains the entire text of James, so a Bible is not absolutely necessary—but each participant will find it useful to have one. You should have at least one Bible on hand for your discussions. (See page 80 for recommendations.)

**How do we get started?** Before you begin, take a look at the suggestions for Bible discussion groups (page 76) or individuals (page 79).

## The Path to Wholeness

### *Introducing the Letter of James*

W hat do you look for in a sermon? I can tell you what I look for. I like the preacher to cut the flowery language and cutesy stories, explain the Scripture, and show how it applies to life today. In a sermon, I'm not looking for sentimental inspirations or flights of theological speculation; I'm looking for insights into what God's word means and how it connects with me.

If your preference in sermons runs toward poems and anecdotes, you may find the letter of James not to your taste. But if you like your sermons plain and direct, then the letter of James is just the sort of thing for you, since that is exactly what the letter of James is: a practical sermon about Christian living.

James's sermon is almost two thousand years old, so we do need a little help to understand it. But it requires less scholarly commentary than many other parts of the Bible. James deals with our struggle to surmount inner conflicts and become whole persons; he shows us how to become men and women of integrity and peace. The relevance of his subject and his straightforward style make James's letter-sermon one of the most accessible portions of the Bible. Although many worthwhile books have been written about James's letter, we don't have to bring a stack of them with us when we sit down to read it.

What we do need to bring is ourselves. James not only points us toward the ideals of Christian life; he peels back the surface of our religious activity to expose the obstacles within us that impede our progress toward these ideals. He invites us to join him in an examination of our values. The primary requirement for benefiting from James's sermon is willingness to take up his invitation.

**A starting point for understanding James's sermon** is to see its connection with the sermons of Jesus. Jesus traveled from town to town in Palestine, announcing to his fellow Jews that God's kingdom—God's life-giving presence and power— was about to arrive and teaching them how to enter this kingdom and live in it. The Palestinian Jews who embraced Jesus as the Messiah, at the time of his preaching or after his death and resurrection, remembered his words and joined together to live them. They formed themselves into local communities that they sometimes called *synagogues*, the Greek term for "assembly" that Jews customarily used. These Jewish-Christian communities were the recipients of James's letter. James, it seems, took up the oral tradition of Jesus' teaching (the written Gospels may not have been composed yet) and addressed these Jewish Christians living in Galilee and in adjacent areas—present-day Lebanon, Syria, and southern Turkey.

If you have done any reading of the New Testament—and even if you haven't—you are probably acquainted with the sermon in which Jesus launched his public ministry: the Sermon on the Mount (Matthew 5–7). From this sermon come such well-known statements and instructions as "Blessed are the poor in spirit" (5:3), "Love your enemies" (5:44), and "Seek first the kingdom of God" (see 6:33). In this hilltop sermon, and in a similar one presented at ground level (the Sermon on the Plain—Luke 6:20–49), Jesus conveyed the basic principles of his way of life. (As they appear in Matthew's and Luke's Gospels, these sermons are probably collections made by Jesus' followers of teachings that he presented in various situations over the course of his ministry.) James's preaching flows directly from these sermons of Jesus. James deals with the same topics that Jesus did, reinforcing certain points and helping his reader-listeners apply the teaching to themselves. Just as Matthew 5–7 is called the Sermon on the Mount and Luke 6:20–49 the Sermon on the Plain, the letter of James might be called the Sermon in the Synagogue (James uses the Greek term *synagogue* for the Christian assembly in 2:2, translated "assembly" by NRSV).

James's sermon resembles Jesus' sermons not only in terms of the topics he deals with but also in terms of a topic he does *not* deal with. In his Sermons on the Mount and on the Plain, Jesus did not speak about his death and resurrection but presented his instructions for how his followers should live. Similarly, James says nothing about Jesus' saving death and resurrection. The Christians to whom James wrote would have been familiar with oral accounts of Jesus' death and resurrection. James's subject, however, is not the meaning of Jesus' death and resurrection but the application of Jesus' teaching about how to live as members of God's kingdom.

**By this point you are probably wondering who this James was.** He calls himself simply "James, a servant of God and of the Lord Jesus Christ" (James 1:1). While this lean statement asserts James's authority as a divinely authorized spokesman, it does not answer our questions about his identity. But this in itself is significant. Only a well-recognized leader would have been able to teach his fellow Christians with such authority without needing to present his credentials. The James who wrote the letter must have been a well-known, widely accepted leader of the early Church. If we look at the several men named James in the New Testament, the outstanding candidate for author of our letter is the one known as "James the Lord's brother" (Galatians 1:19; see Mark 6:1–3). In fact, the letter of James has been attributed to this James through most of Christian history.

In Aramaic, the language spoken by Jews in Palestine at the time of Jesus, the word for "brother" covers a wider range of family relationships than does the word *brother* in English. The Aramaic word for "brother" may denote not only a sibling but another male relative—a cousin, an uncle, etc. Since it was in Aramaic that James was first called the "Lord's brother," this identification does not necessarily mean that he was a full brother of Jesus. Thus his title does not stand in contradiction to the Church's teaching that Mary remained a virgin after Jesus' birth and had no other children. James and Jesus were probably cousins in some degree.

None of Jesus' male relatives followed him during his earthly life (John 7:5), but some became his followers after his resurrection (Acts 1:14). Paul records that Jesus made a special appearance to James after rising from the dead (1 Corinthians 15:7). When Peter, the first leader of the church in Jerusalem, began to travel extensively, James took over the leadership of the Jerusalem community, which was the center of the early Christian movement. In Jerusalem, James presided over the first—and arguably the most crucial—council in the history of the Church (Acts 15). Jews outside the Christian community honored him with the title "James the Just," that is, James the Righteous, for his upright life in obedience to the Mosaic law. But his position of leadership in the Christian community made him an object of hostility to Jewish leaders who regarded Christianity as a dangerous deviation within Judaism. In the year 62, James's opponents brought about his death. Thus the letter we are about to read comes from the earliest period of the life of the Church, probably some time in the 40s or 50s.

I should mention that there is a range of scholarly opinion on the authorship and date of the letter of James. Since the letter is written in a more fluent Greek than might be expected of someone from a small village in Galilee, some experts view it as the product of an unknown later author who used James's name, and perhaps some of James's material. But the traditional view that the author was James the Lord's brother is maintained by some scholars today, and that view will be the basis of our discussion in this booklet.

What about the people to whom James wrote: what do we know about them? Historians have devoted considerable attention to earliest Jewish Christianity, but they are unable to draw a detailed picture of the letter's recipients. From James's letter itself we get a very general impression of them. The way he speaks of the preciousness of the harvest (5:7) suggests that his readers were small-scale farmers, for whom every fruit tree and stalk of grain made a difference. It is impossible to determine the recipients' economic and political situation with precision, but apparently some of them were being exploited by wealthy, powerful people (2:6–7; 5:1–6). An occasional wealthy person, and probably more than an occasional indigent person, could be seen in their assembly (2:1–7). One thing we know for sure: these early Christians were not yet thoroughly transformed by Jesus' teaching. Their hearts were still divided between the values of the world and the values of God's kingdom. Jesus' way of life was only gradually taking root in their lives. In this respect, they were much like us, despite considerable cultural and social differences.

**A few of James's concepts deserve a brief introduction.** James speaks of "the word of truth" (1:18), "the implanted word" (1:21), "the perfect law" (1:25), "the law of liberty" (1:25; 2:12), "the royal law" (2:8), and simply "the law" (2:9, 11; 4:11). With various nuances, all these terms refer to the moral law that God gave to his people Israel, as interpreted by Jesus, who focused on the central requirements of mercy and love (2:8). Jesus' Sermon on the Mount provides a good idea of what James means by God's "word" or "law." In James's mind, the law is not a burdensome set of rules but God's call to imitate his love (see 1:27). God's word, or law, brings freedom because it contains a power that transforms us as we respond to it (1:21).

Like the other authors of the New Testament, James speaks of "faith" as our response to God's life-giving word. As you will see, James thinks of faith as a compound—a combination of belief plus action. When you come to the word in your reading of James, try mentally translating it as "firmly committed believing" or "faith in action."

James also uses the term "works" (2:14–26), which could lead to a misunderstanding. When James speaks of the insufficiency of faith without "works," it may seem that he is arguing against St. Paul's teaching that we are saved not by works but by faith (Romans 3:21–4:25; Galatians 2:15–3:14). On closer reading, however, it seems less clear that James is taking issue with Paul. Paul speaks of "works *of the law*" (see Romans 3:20, 28; Galatians 2:16; 3:2, 10), by which he means especially certain ceremonial aspects of the Mosaic law, such as circumcision, which mark Jews as distinct from non-Jews. Paul argued that our relationship with God depends not on observance of these works of the law but on faith in Jesus. James, however, speaks not of "works of the law" but simply of "works," by which he means actively following the way of life that lies at the heart of the Mosaic law as interpreted by Jesus. Paul would agree with James that we cannot have a relationship with God if we violate the basic requirements of justice and mercy

(Galatians 5:19–21). James never argues that we are set right with God by our deeds *rather* than by faith. His argument is that faith and faithful actions cannot be separated. Without the deeds of love that spring from faith, faith is not really faith at all. Thus I would make another suggestion: when you come to the term "works" in James, mentally translate it as "actions motivated by faith" or "active expressions of faith."

**We will begin our exploration of James's letter in a leisurely way,** with shorter readings in the first three weeks to allow us the opportunity to become familiar with his characteristic ideas. Along with the readings from James, I have included additional passages from Scripture, mainly from Jesus' preaching, that deal with subjects that James treats. I have not discussed these non-Jamesian excerpts in the "Guide to the Reading" sections, although some of the questions for careful reading and questions for application refer to them. Finally, let me point out that I have often written that James speaks *to us,* even though, strictly speaking, he wrote his letter not to us but to some of our long-deceased Christian brothers and sisters in the ancient Near East. By the grace of God, the letter is so relevant today, even after twenty centuries, that it seems natural to say simply that James speaks to us. James's words to his recipients are God's words to us.

As I already suggested, what we get out of James's letter depends on what we put into it. James's message is directed to adults and to those who want to become adults, because it concerns responsibility. He calls us to respond to God's presence in our lives. James's letter provides us not with a theology of Christ but with a call to examine ourselves as Christ's disciples; thus reading it is an opportunity to learn, but mostly about ourselves. Are we willing to submit our hearts to God (see 4:7–10) so that we can love God wholeheartedly? James would say that reading his letter and failing to act on it is not reading it at all. On the other hand, "those who look into the perfect law, the law of liberty, and persevere, being not hearers who forget but doers who act—they will be blessed in their doing" (1:25; references in this booklet are to the letter of James unless otherwise noted).

# MATURITY, ANYONE?

## Questions to Begin

*15 minutes*
*Use a question or two to get warmed up for the reading.*

**1** In the last week, what made you happy?

**2** What's your favorite flower? Why do you like it?

## Opening the Bible

*5 minutes*
*Read the passage aloud. Let individuals take turns reading paragraphs.*

## The Reading: James 1:1–11

### Faith Grows amid Hardships

1 James, a servant of God and of the Lord Jesus Christ,
    To the twelve tribes in the Dispersion:
    Greetings.
    2 My brothers and sisters, whenever you face trials of any kind, consider it nothing but joy, 3 because you know that the testing of your faith produces endurance; 4 and let endurance have its full effect, so that you may be mature and complete, lacking in nothing.
    5 If any of you is lacking in wisdom, ask God, who gives to all generously and ungrudgingly, and it will be given you. 6 But ask in faith, never doubting, for the one who doubts is like a wave of the sea, driven and tossed by the wind; 7, 8 for the doubter, being double-minded and unstable in every way, must not expect to receive anything from the Lord.

### Adjust Your Worldview

9 Let the believer who is lowly boast in being raised up, 10 and the rich in being brought low, because the rich will disappear like a flower in the field. 11 For the sun rises with its scorching heat and withers the field; its flower falls, and its beauty perishes. It is the same way with the rich; in the midst of a busy life, they will wither away.

## Supplementary Readings

### Who Will Be Happy? (Matthew 5:1–10)

1 When Jesus saw the crowds, he went up the mountain; and after he sat down, his disciples came to him. 2 Then he began to speak, and taught them, saying:
    3 "Blessed are the poor in spirit, for theirs is the kingdom of heaven.
    4 "Blessed are those who mourn, for they will be comforted.
    5 "Blessed are the meek, for they will inherit the earth.
    6 "Blessed are those who hunger and thirst for righteousness, for they will be filled.

7 "Blessed are the merciful, for they will receive mercy.

8 "Blessed are the pure in heart, for they will see God.

9 "Blessed are the peacemakers, for they will be called children of God.

10 "Blessed are those who are persecuted for righteousness' sake, for theirs is the kingdom of heaven."

## Which Will You Choose? (Matthew 6:19–21, 24)

19 Do not store up for yourselves treasures on earth, where moth and rust consume and where thieves break in and steal; 20 but store up for yourselves treasures in heaven, where neither moth nor rust consumes and where thieves do not break in and steal. 21 For where your treasure is, there your heart will be also. . . . 24 No one can serve two masters; for a slave will either hate the one and love the other, or be devoted to the one and despise the other. You cannot serve God and wealth.

## Questions for Careful Reading

*10 minutes*
*Choose questions according to your interest and time.*

**1** If James is "the Lord's brother," why doesn't he identify himself this way (1:1)?

**2** What does James mean by "joy" (1:2)?

**3** What kind of wisdom does James seem to have in mind in verse 5?

**4** Which of Jesus' beatitudes ("Blessed are . . . "—Matthew 5:3–10) have some connection to the reading from James? How does each passage help us understand the other?

**5** What are the similarities and differences between James 1:9–11 and Matthew 6:19–21, 24?

## A Guide to the Reading

*If participants have not read this section already, read it aloud. Otherwise go on to "Questions for Application."*

**1:1–4.** James urges us to take a patient attitude toward suffering. He bases his encouragement on an unstated assumption, and it will benefit us to bring it out into the open. To refer to the distresses of life as "trials" assumes that human life is not a mere sequence of random happenings but a meaningful process with a specific goal. In this process a divine Trainer is with us, ready to use everything, especially our hardships and sorrows, to test us and challenge us to grow. James recognizes that at present we are immature and incomplete persons, but he is confident that with our Trainer's help we can become fully developed, men and women of integrity and wholeness, "lacking in nothing." James's outlook on life can be a source of joy alongside even the deepest sorrow, not because it anesthetizes our pain but because it gives us hope that no matter how chaotic or incomprehensible our suffering may be, it is not ultimately useless or absurd.

How does this training process work? James tells us that "endurance" of suffering is a vital factor in our development. By reminding us that life is transitory, suffering spurs us to turn to God, who is eternal. At the same time, because suffering seems to call God's love into question, it challenges us to reaffirm our trust in God. Thus our relationship with God deepens under stress. We grow to maturity as men and women of truth and love by holding on to God's truth and love even in adverse circumstances—just as an athlete grows to excellence through workouts and competition.

James's words spur me to examine my own attitude toward my problems. Do I worry? feel envious of those who have an easier life? become discouraged? You bet I do. God has a vision of my becoming a complete person, and he views my difficulties as chances for me to get closer to that goal; but I fixate on the bad news in today's memo, report card, diagnosis, or tax notice. How differently God and I look at my problems!

**1:5–8.** In order to undergo trials in a spirit of submission to God, we need insight into God's plans: a sense that God's power is active on our behalf, that God overcomes evil with good, that God is leading us through transitory earthly life toward an eternal kingdom. James calls this insight "wisdom," and he declares that God is unhesitatingly willing to give it to us.

However, we must ask for this wisdom "in faith, never doubting." The Greek word translated "doubting" also means hesitating, being at odds with oneself, being undecided. The old Catholic translation brought out this meaning by rendering James's words: "Ask in faith, nothing wavering." James's point is that we must seek God's wisdom with a willingness to adopt his values and act on his instructions. The "doubting" that gets in the way of our receiving God's wisdom is not so much our doubt that he will answer our prayer as our doubt as to whether we *want* him to answer it. God is like a coach who is willing to work patiently with an athlete but who challenges the athlete to give the training his or her full effort. The coach knows that if the athlete is not committed, the training won't succeed.

Some of us have not made up our minds. We are "double-minded" and "unstable," or vacillating. James will have much to say to us in his letter.

**1:9–11.** The believer that James calls "lowly" is literally poor, and apparently there are many poor "brothers and sisters" in the Christian communities to which James is writing. In James's view, poverty has an advantage, inasmuch as the poor may have a high place in God's kingdom (1:9). The problem with wealth is that there is no future in it. James's perspective here is an example of the heavenly wisdom of which he has just spoken (1:5). This wisdom reverses the ordinary way of looking at things. It perceives that neither poverty and suffering nor prosperity and ease are what they appear. God has a special love for the poor, while the wealthy are constantly in danger of relying on their material resources rather than on God. The wisdom James speaks of is the kind of wisdom that Mary expressed when she sang that God has "brought down the powerful from their thrones, and lifted up the lowly" (Luke 1:52). This wisdom can sustain us in suffering.

## Questions for Application

*40 minutes*
*Choose questions according to your interest and time.*

| | | |
|---|---|---|
| | **1** | What has James said so far that challenges your thinking? |
| | **2** | What is the greatest difficulty that you are facing? Do you feel angry at God for allowing it? If so, do you talk to God about it? How could you seek God's wisdom for dealing with this situation? |
| | **3** | How can you encourage others in your church community to have faith in God when they are experiencing difficulties or are in pain? |

**4** What experiences have helped you to realize the transitoriness of life?

**5** What need or lack do you experience to which you might apply James's words about being "lowly," or needy (1:9)? What would his words mean for you?

**6** In what ways are you rich? How might you relate to this wealth differently if you viewed it in light of James's words in 1:10–11?

**Without prayer or homework the sense of personal growth or divine communion will fade; without good leaders and a strict schedule, the group will appear to be out of control.**

Jerome Kodell, O.S.B., *The Catholic Bible Study Handbook*

## Approach to Prayer

*15 minutes*
*Use this approach—or create your own!*

---

◆ Read James 1:9–11 aloud. Pause for silent reflection. Then pray together this portion of Mary's Magnificat (Luke 1:46–55). End with a Glory to the Father.

My soul magnifies the Lord,
    and my spirit rejoices in God
        my Savior,
for he has looked with favor on
        the lowliness of his servant.
    Surely, from now on all
        generations will call me
        blessed;
for the Mighty One has done
        great things for me,
    and holy is his name.
His mercy is for those who fear
        him
    from generation to generation.
He has shown strength with his
        arm;
    he has scattered the proud in
        the thoughts of their hearts.
He has brought down the
        powerful from their thrones,
    and lifted up the lowly;
he has filled the hungry with
        good things,
    and sent the rich away empty.
He has helped his servant Israel,
    in remembrance of his mercy,
according to the promise he
        made to our ancestors,
    to Abraham and to his
        descendants forever.

## A Living Tradition

### A Medieval Interpreter's Comments

*This section is a supplement for individual reading.*

The following comments on this week's reading come from Bede, an English monk and scholar who lived in the eighth century and is regarded as a saint (often he is called the Venerable Bede).

**"If any of you is lacking in wisdom, ask God"** (1:5). James seems to be speaking in particular about that wisdom which is indispensable when we face temptations. If any of you cannot understand the usefulness of the temptations which happen to believers in order to test them, he says, ask God that you might be given a mind able to discern the great kindness by which the Father disciplines the children whom he is carefully making worthy of an eternal inheritance (see Proverbs 3:11–12).

**"The doubter, being double-minded . . . must not expect to receive anything from the Lord"** (1:7–8). The double-minded person does not seek an interior reward but external approval for the good things he or she does. . . . People like that are inconsistent in all their ways, because they are both very easily discouraged by the difficulties of the world and entangled by favorable circumstances, so that they turn aside from the true path.

**"Let . . . the rich [boast] in being brought low"** (1:9–10). Clearly this is said with irony. James says, let him remember that his arrogant self-confidence, by which he takes pride in his wealth and looks down on or even oppresses the poor, must come to an end.

**"The rich will disappear like a flower in the field"** (1:10). Wildflowers are delightful in fragrance and appearance, but they very quickly lose the charm of their beauty and sweetness. Therefore the present happiness of the wicked, which cannot last very long, is quite rightly compared to them.

**"In the midst of a busy life, [the rich] will wither away"** (1:11). He is not speaking about every wealthy person but the one who trusts in uncertain riches. For by contrasting a wealthy person with a poor brother or sister, he shows that he is talking about the wealthy person who is not humble. . . . Such a wealthy person, that is, one who is proud and wicked and prefers earthly joys to heavenly ones, will wither away in the midst of a busy life, perishing in the midst of evil actions because he or she has passed up the opportunity to enter the Lord's straight way.

# Be Blessed in Your Doing

## Questions to Begin

*15 minutes*
*Use a question or two to get warmed up for the reading.*

---

**1**  Describe a memorable gift that you have received. What made it special?

---

**2**  Who in your life is (or was) a good listener? What do you (or did you) like to talk about with that person?

*5 minutes*
*Read the passage aloud. Let individuals take turns reading
paragraphs.*

## The Reading: James 1:12–27

### Take Responsibility

12 Blessed is anyone who endures temptation. Such a one has stood
the test and will receive the crown of life that the Lord has promised
to those who love him. 13 No one, when tempted, should say, "I am
being tempted by God"; for God cannot be tempted by evil and he
himself tempts no one. 14 But one is tempted by one's own desire,
being lured and enticed by it; 15 then, when that desire has conceived,
it gives birth to sin, and that sin, when it is fully grown, gives birth to
death.

### Take God's Grace

16 Do not be deceived, my beloved.

17 Every generous act of giving, with every perfect gift, is from
above, coming down from the Father of lights, with whom there is no
variation or shadow due to change. 18 In fulfillment of his own
purpose he gave us birth by the word of truth, so that we would
become a kind of first fruits of his creatures.

19 You must understand this, my beloved: let everyone be quick to
listen, slow to speak, slow to anger; 20 for your anger does not
produce God's righteousness. 21 Therefore rid yourselves of all
sordidness and rank growth of wickedness, and welcome with
meekness the implanted word that has the power to save your souls.

### Take Action

22 But be doers of the word, and not merely hearers who deceive
themselves. 23 For if any are hearers of the word and not doers, they
are like those who look at themselves in a mirror; 24 for they look at
themselves and, on going away, immediately forget what they were
like. 25 But those who look into the perfect law, the law of liberty, and
persevere, being not hearers who forget but doers who act—they will
be blessed in their doing.

26 If any think they are religious, and do not bridle their tongues
but deceive their hearts, their religion is worthless. 27 Religion that is
pure and undefiled before God, the Father, is this: to care for orphans

and widows in their distress, and to keep oneself unstained by the
world.


## Supplementary Reading

### If You Need God's Help (Luke 11:9–13)

9 I say to you, Ask, and it will be given you; search, and you will find;
knock, and the door will be opened for you. 10 For everyone who
asks receives, and everyone who searches finds, and for everyone who
knocks, the door will be opened. 11 Is there anyone among you who,
if your child asks for a fish, will give a snake instead of a fish? 12 Or if
the child asks for an egg, will give a scorpion? 13 If you then, who are
evil, know how to give good gifts to your children, how much more
will the heavenly Father give the Holy Spirit to those who ask him!

*10 minutes*
*Choose questions according to your interest and time.*

**1** How is sin connected with death (1:15)?

**2** Why can God's law be compared to a mirror (1:23–24)?

**3** Compare the imagery concerning God's word in 1:18 with that in 1:21. What different aspects of God's word do the images bring out?

**4** Why does James single out the particular kinds of behavior that he mentions in 1:26–27?

**5** How might Jesus' words in Luke 11:9–13 shed light on James's words in 1:17?

**6** In a sentence or two, how would you sum up James's message in this reading?

## A Guide to the Reading

*If participants have not read this section already, read it aloud. Otherwise go on to "Questions for Application."*

**1:12–15.** James offers more of the wisdom (1:5) that enables us to approach our trials with a constructive attitude. God's wisdom enables us to direct our lives toward the ultimate purpose that he has created us for—"the crown of life," that is, eternal life with God. Enduring temptation—bearing up under trials and resisting temptation—moves us toward this goal.

Of course, along the way we often fall and need God's forgiveness. James emphasizes that we must take responsibility for our moral failures. While God does sometimes *test* us by letting us undergo trials (Genesis 22:1; Psalm 26:2), he does not *tempt* us in the sense of luring us toward evil (Genesis 3:1–7). When I fail, it is not because of God's testing but because of my own self-centeredness and inner conflict. I am divided within myself, ambivalent, torn between noble aspirations and selfish desires (see Romans 7:14–25). If I refuse to take responsibility for my moral failures, I will never overcome this inner dividedness.

**1:16–21.** James has urged us to avoid evil (1:12–15), and shortly he will urge us to do good (1:22–27). Here, in the center of his appeal, he speaks about God's grace—God's freely given help—because grace is central. Only with God's power can we turn from sin and grow in love.

We may be double-minded, wavering between good and evil, but God is unwavering. God is the giver of good things. He single-mindedly pursues what is good for us. He has given us his divine life by his word of truth (James's female imagery for God is notable: God has given birth to us—1:18). By the "word of truth" James means Jesus' teaching about leading a life of humility, love, and peace (Matthew 5–7; Luke 6:20–49). This divinely given word will save us (1:21).

Thus "let everyone be quick to listen" (1:19) is not general advice about being good listeners. James is urging us to pay attention specifically to God's word. Likewise, James is not just advising us to keep our tempers under control when he tells us to be "slow to anger" (1:19); he is advising us to put aside our bitterness at God for allowing us to suffer (for example, the anger expressed in the protest in 1:13—"I am being tempted by God").

Grumbling against God is the opposite of submitting humbly to his will. As St. Paul wrote, "Do all things without murmuring and arguing, so that you may be blameless and innocent, children of God without blemish" (Philippians 2:14–15).

James tells us to rid ourselves of evil (1:21)—to overcome our inner conflict by rejecting sin, to abandon double-mindedness and move toward wholeness. He advocates a vigorous cooperation with God's grace. God's grace will save us (1:21)—but only as we *use* it to struggle against our sinful tendencies.

**1:22–27.** James warns us not to deceive ourselves about hearing God's word. If you hear God's word and don't respond, James declares, you have not heard. To be "merely hearers" is to not really be hearers at all.

James calls God's law "the perfect law" (1:25), which means that it is complete. It is complete because it is the path to becoming a complete human being. If I follow the law of love as taught by Jesus, I will ultimately become a whole person. Thus, in a sense, God's law provides a picture of mature, complete human life. The person who looks at that picture and then lives according to it will attain "liberty" (1:25)—the freedom that comes from knowing one's goal in life and moving toward it, with God's help.

Hearers only, by contrast, end up contradicting themselves. I hear God's word and agree with it—yet I do not act on it. I am full of religious talk—but also uncharitable talk (1:26). I have faith—but I don't express it in care for the needy (the first half of 1:27). I am a churchgoer—but worldly values shape how I relate to other people (the second half of 1:27). In reverse order, these three problems will be James's topics in our next readings (worldliness, 2:1–13; failure to care for the needy, 2:14–26; uncharitable speech, 3:1–12).

James holds before us the prospect of living a life of integrity, of overcoming the conflict of desires and values within us. And he points out the way to this personal integrity. We will find personal wholeness by practicing a religion that is whole—by living according to "religion that is pure and undefiled" (1:27). This pure religion is, in brief, devoting oneself to those who are in need.

## Questions for Application

*40 minutes*
*Choose questions according to your interest and time.*

**1** In your personal experience, who has exemplified perseverance? What can you learn from their example?

**2** Where in your life do you need a spirit of perseverance?

**3** In the ancient world, orphans and widows were often unable to provide for their own needs and could not adequately protect themselves. Who are the "orphans and widows" of modern society?

**4** Those who blame God for their hardships (1:13) view their difficulties in a different way than those who find a reason for joy in the midst of their hardships (1:2). Why do people react to suffering in such different ways?

**5** Reread 1:19–20. Is there a healthy way of being angry with God? Consider Psalms 10, 13, and 44.

**6** In your attempt to live according to God's word, when have you experienced God's help?

**7** Why does James lay such an emphasis on the danger of self-deception (1:16, 22)?

**Study your heart in the light of holy Scripture and you will know therein who you were, who you are, and who you ought to be.**

Fulgentius of Ruspe, Letter to Theodore

## Approach to Prayer

*15 minutes*
*Use this approach—or create your own!*

◆ Pray this portion of Psalm 19 together. End with an Our Father.

The law of the LORD is perfect,
   reviving the soul;
the decrees of the LORD are sure,
   making wise the simple;
the precepts of the LORD are right,
   rejoicing the heart. . . .
More to be desired are they than
     gold,
   even much fine gold;
sweeter also than honey,
   and drippings of the
     honeycomb.

Moreover by them is your
     servant warned;
   in keeping them there is great
     reward.
But who can detect their errors?
   Clear me from hidden
     faults. . . .
Then I shall be blameless,
   and innocent of great
     transgression.

Let the words of my mouth and
     the meditation of my heart
   be acceptable to you,
   O LORD, my rock and my
     redeemer.

## Saints in the Making

### *Look at Yourself in the Mirror*

*This section is a supplement for individual reading.*

James speaks of hearing God's word but then forgetting it, an action similar to glancing at ourselves in a mirror but then forgetting what we look like (1:23–24). How can we avoid this danger? The nineteenth-century Danish Lutheran philosopher Søren Kierkegaard made this question the subject of a somewhat dour but thought-provoking essay, "What Is Required to Look at Oneself with True Blessing in the Mirror of the Word?"

The first requirement, Kierkegaard writes, is that you must not look at the mirror but at yourself in the mirror. An immense scholarly literature has grown up around the Bible, and you can spend a lifetime reading commentaries about it while never really reading it as God's personal word to you. To read *about* the Bible may be useful, Kierkegaard observed, but it is not the same thing as reading the Bible as God's word to you.

The second requirement for seeing yourself in the mirror of God's word is to constantly tell yourself, "It is speaking about me." For example, when reading Jesus' parable of the good Samaritan (Luke 10:25–37) and coming to the part about the priest who passes by the injured man, Kierkegaard suggests that you say, "This priest is myself. Alas, to think I could be so callous, I who call myself a Christian." When you come to the Levite, "Here you shall say, 'It is I—oh, to think, when it has already happened to me once, that I could be so hard of heart that the same thing could happen to me even a second time, that I have not become any better!'" When, however, you come to the compassionate Samaritan, "lest you become weary of incessantly saying, 'It is I,' for a change you may here say, 'It was not I—ah, no, I am not like that!'"

The final requirement, Kierkegaard writes, is to remember what you have seen of yourself in the mirror of God's word at least today, at least for an hour. In Kierkegaard's view, it is self-deceiving to promise yourself that you will remember for a lifetime and yet forget today. Rather than being like a chronic gambler who tells himself that he will "give up gambling after tonight," you should be like the gambler who says to himself, "I may be a gambler for the rest of my days, but at least *tonight* I am going to leave it alone."

# NOT SEEING AS THE WORLD SEES

## Question to Begin

*15 minutes*
*Use this question to get warmed up for the reading.*

---

**1** Describe a situation in which you were self-conscious about your clothes or were surprised by the way someone else was dressed.

**When in the moments of leisure and reflection you take up the sacred book, be impressed with the conviction that you then converse with God himself; commence therefore by prayer, to obtain that it may be to you a lamp to guide your feet in safety through the shades of this valley of death.**

Bishops of the United States, First Provincial Council of Baltimore, 1829

*5 minutes*
*Read the passage aloud. Let individuals take turns reading paragraphs.*

## The Reading: James 2:1–13

### What Would Jesus Do?

1 My brothers and sisters, do you with your acts of favoritism really believe in our glorious Lord Jesus Christ? 2 For if a person with gold rings and in fine clothes comes into your assembly, and if a poor person in dirty clothes also comes in, 3 and if you take notice of the one wearing the fine clothes and say, "Have a seat here, please," while to the one who is poor you say, "Stand there," or, "Sit at my feet," 4 have you not made distinctions among yourselves, and become judges with evil thoughts? 5 Listen, my beloved brothers and sisters. Has not God chosen the poor in the world to be rich in faith and to be heirs of the kingdom that he has promised to those who love him? 6 But you have dishonored the poor. Is it not the rich who oppress you? Is it not they who drag you into court? 7 Is it not they who blaspheme the excellent name that was invoked over you?

8 You do well if you really fulfill the royal law according to the scripture, "You shall love your neighbor as yourself." 9 But if you show partiality, you commit sin and are convicted by the law as transgressors. 10 For whoever keeps the whole law but fails in one point has become accountable for all of it. 11 For the one who said, "You shall not commit adultery," also said, "You shall not murder." Now if you do not commit adultery but if you murder, you have become a transgressor of the law. 12 So speak and so act as those who are to be judged by the law of liberty. 13 For judgment will be without mercy to anyone who has shown no mercy; mercy triumphs over judgment.

## Supplementary Readings

### Love Does Not Seek Its Own Advantage (Luke 6:31–36)

31 Do to others as you would have them do to you.

32 If you love those who love you, what credit is that to you? For even sinners love those who love them. 33 If you do good to those who do good to you, what credit is that to you? For even sinners do the same. 34 If you lend to those from whom you hope to receive,

what credit is that to you? Even sinners lend to sinners, to receive as much again. 35 But love your enemies, do good, and lend, expecting nothing in return. Your reward will be great, and you will be children of the Most High; for he is kind to the ungrateful and the wicked. 36 Be merciful, just as your Father is merciful.

## Love Does Not Expect a Return (Luke 14:12–14)

12 When you give a luncheon or a dinner, do not invite your friends or your brothers or your relatives or rich neighbors, in case they may invite you in return, and you would be repaid. 13 But when you give a banquet, invite the poor, the crippled, the lame, and the blind. 14 And you will be blessed, because they cannot repay you, for you will be repaid at the resurrection of the righteous.

*10 minutes*
*Choose questions according to your interest and time.*

**1** What contemporary example of favoritism might James point to if he were writing today?

**2** Is the behavior described in 2:2–3 an expression of love for the wealthy person?

**3** Why is favoritism against the law of love (2:8–9)?

**4** What do James's comparisons in 2:11 indicate about the seriousness with which he views partiality?

**5** How might Jesus' words in Luke 6:33–34 and 14:12 help us understand why the believers treat the wealthy person as they do in James 2:2–3?

## A Guide to the Reading

*If participants have not read this section already, read it aloud. Otherwise go on to "Questions for Application."*

**2:1.** At the end of last week's reading James spoke about keeping ourselves "unstained by the world" (1:27). The worldliness he had in mind was not visiting pornographic Web sites but evaluating people according to their income.

The Greek words translated "do you with your acts of favoritism really believe in our glorious Lord Jesus Christ?" do not necessarily express a question. They could also be rendered as an instruction: "Do not hold the faith of our glorious Lord Jesus Christ with acts of partiality." Here "the faith of Jesus Christ" may mean not faith *in* Jesus but the kind of faith that Jesus taught and exemplified. James's point, it seems, is that we should not try to mix Jesus' way of life, Jesus' values, with a worldly outlook and worldly values. Showing partiality is not what Jesus taught or how he lived. He welcomed all people equally, regardless of their reputation or social standing.

**2:2–4.** The incident with the rich man\* and the poor man is probably the sort of thing that happened often (2:6 treats it as a fact). In the ancient world, even more than today, getting ahead depended on who you knew. People naturally gravitated toward the wealthy and influential (see Luke 6:32–34; 14:12).

Notice the emphasis on outward impressions (2:2). The well-dressed man is obviously a person of distinction. You know right away that you could benefit from being associated with him. The other man is dressed shabbily; if you are concerned about your reputation you would do best not to give the impression that he is your friend. Yet how wrong it is that members of the church should evaluate each other by the same outward appearances that the world pays attention to rather than according to their inner worth in God's eyes.

James puts his finger on our attempt to live by contradictory value systems—that of the world and that of God. The different welcomes given to the rich man and the poor man manifest the problem of double-mindedness. It is a matter of loving God yet also loving status and honor. James says this double-mindedness makes us "judges with evil thoughts," that is, people who judge by false

\* NRSV translates the Greek word for *man* as "person."

standards. We evaluate people falsely because we view their importance as proportionate to the kind of car they drive or the size of the house they live in.

**2:5–7.** God, rather than favoring the rich, has shown a preferential love for the poor by making poverty a gateway through which the gift of faith can flow. A young friend of mine recently returned from a trip to Kenya. She was impressed by the many poor people she met there whose faith was more joyful than that of most Christians she knows at home. But we don't have to travel to Africa to find poor people who are wealthy in their trust in God and in their generosity to those who are in even greater need.

James does not say that the church community neglects the poor man's material needs. Perhaps they give him a handout at the end of the service. But because of his poverty, he is deprived of respect in the eyes of the group (2:3, 6).

**2:8–11.** God commanded, "You shall love your neighbor as yourself" (Leviticus 19:18). Jesus identified this command, along with love of God, as the central principle of the kingdom of God (Matthew 22:36–40). Thus it is the "royal law"—the law of the kingdom. When James speaks of keeping the "whole law" (2:10), he does not mean observing all the details of the Mosaic law but carrying out this law of love of neighbor consistently. Showing partiality to the wealthy violates this law, for it entails treating the poor as less deserving of honor. This inconsistency was already condemned in the Old Testament, in which God not only said do not murder or commit adultery but also said, "You shall not be partial to the poor or defer to the great" (Leviticus 19:15).

**2:12–13.** James calls this standard by which God will ultimately judge us "the law of liberty." We might even call it the law of mercy: "Be merciful, just as your Father is merciful" (Luke 6:36). Jesus teaches us to redirect our energies from self-aggrandizement to compassion for our fellow human beings. His teaching is "the implanted word that has the power to save your souls" (1:21). If we let mercy overcome our self-centered tendencies, God's grace will heal our divided hearts, and we will have no need to fear God's judgment (Matthew 25:31–46).

## Questions for Application

*40 minutes*
*Choose questions according to your interest and time.*

**1** What effect does partiality have in a family? in a parish? at a job site?

**2** Why is faith in God sometimes stronger among people who live in poverty than among those who are wealthy?

**3** Does our nation's foreign policy devote adequate attention to poorer and needier countries? If not, why are they neglected? What are the effects of this problem? What could be done about it?

**4** In what ways do business, politics, and the media promote the attitude that wealthy people are more important than poor people? In what ways are you influenced by this attitude?

**5** James touches on the human tendency to make distinctions between rich people and poor people. What other distinctions between people do we tend to make in modern society? How do these distinctions square with Jesus' way of valuing people?

**6** What could you do this week to translate kind words into helpful action for someone in need?

**7** How can you build your local church community into a place where people can unlearn worldly ways of valuing each other?

## Approach to Prayer

*15 minutes*
*Use this approach—or create your own!*

---

◆ Read aloud Matthew 25:31–46. Pause for silent reflection. Then pray together the following prayer. Close with an Our Father.

Lord and giver of life, you have created each person in your own image and likeness. Open our eyes to see your image in each person we meet. Lord of mercy without limit, help us to recognize the opportunities you give us to show compassion to others.

## Saints in the Making

### Showing Respect

*This section is a supplement for individual reading.*

When the youngest of her twelve children started school, Mary Jo Copeland began to volunteer at Catholic Charities in Minneapolis. Impatient with government regulations that affected the agency's activities, however, she sought another outlet for her energies. In 1985 she opened a storefront center for the hungry called Sharing and Caring Hands. Over the next three years, the center's services expanded. When the shelter was forced to move because of city redevelopment plans, Copeland purchased and renovated a downtown building with almost $1 million that she had raised through constant speaking at churches and civic organizations. In 1992, Copeland—called a "one-woman fund-raising machine" by one journalist—raised several million dollars and bought a plot of land next to Sharing and Caring Hands. Here she built a residential shelter called Mary's Place for homeless individuals and families.

By the beginning of 2000, Sharing and Caring Hands was serving meals to more than a thousand people a day. With more than ninety units, Mary's Place was providing housing for more than five hundred people. The work was carried out by some thirty volunteers and more than a dozen salaried staff. (Mary Jo Copeland is not on the payroll, although her husband, Dick Copeland, is salaried as the general manager.)

One of the project's most striking features is the respect its staff shows to those who are served. The residential units are kept clean. Each child has his or her own solid-wood bunk bed. Twice a day Copeland puts on rubber gloves, gets down on the floor, and washes the feet of the homeless people who happen to be sitting in the shelter's main room. She applies a little soothing ointment to sore spots, gives a pair of new socks to those who need them, and then invites them to pray with her.

James reproached his listeners for treating with disrespect the raggedly clothed people who came into their assembly. "You have dishonored the poor," he declared indignantly (2:6). If he were to visit Sharing and Caring Hands, he might say, "You have not only helped people in need but have treated them with the dignity they deserve."

# Is Your Faith "Out of Order"?

## Questions to Begin

*15 minutes*
*Use a question or two to get warmed up for the reading.*

**1** What is the most frustrating problem you've ever had with a piece of equipment or machinery?

**2** Recall an amusing slip of the tongue that you made or heard someone else make.

*5 minutes*
*Read the passage aloud. Let individuals take turns reading*
*paragraphs.*

## The Reading: James 2:14–3:12

### Real Faith Takes Action

14 What good is it, my brothers and sisters, if you say you have faith but do not have works? Can faith save you? 15 If a brother or sister is naked and lacks daily food, 16 and one of you says to them, "Go in peace; keep warm and eat your fill," and yet you do not supply their bodily needs, what is the good of that? 17 So faith by itself, if it has no works, is dead.

18 But someone will say, "You have faith and I have works." Show me your faith apart from your works, and I by my works will show you my faith. 19 You believe that God is one; you do well. Even the demons believe—and shudder. 20 Do you want to be shown, you senseless person, that faith apart from works is barren? 21 Was not our ancestor Abraham justified by works when he offered his son Isaac on the altar? 22 You see that faith was active along with his works, and faith was brought to completion by the works. 23 Thus the scripture was fulfilled that says, "Abraham believed God, and it was reckoned to him as righteousness," and he was called the friend of God. 24 You see that a person is justified by works and not by faith alone. 25 Likewise, was not Rahab the prostitute also justified by works when she welcomed the messengers and sent them out by another road? 26 For just as the body without the spirit is dead, so faith without works is also dead.

### The Almost Untamable Tongue

3:1 Not many of you should become teachers, my brothers and sisters, for you know that we who teach will be judged with greater strictness. 2 For all of us make many mistakes. Anyone who makes no mistakes in speaking is perfect, able to keep the whole body in check with a bridle. 3 If we put bits into the mouths of horses to make them obey us, we guide their whole bodies. 4 Or look at ships: though they are so large that it takes strong winds to drive them, yet they are guided by a very small rudder wherever the will of the pilot directs. 5 So also the tongue is a small member, yet it boasts of great exploits.

How great a forest is set ablaze by a small fire! 6 And the tongue is a fire. The tongue is placed among our members as a world of iniquity; it stains the whole body, sets on fire the cycle of nature, and is itself set on fire by hell. 7 For every species of beast and bird, of reptile and sea creature, can be tamed and has been tamed by the human species, 8 but no one can tame the tongue—a restless evil, full of deadly poison. 9 With it we bless the Lord and Father, and with it we curse those who are made in the likeness of God. 10 From the same mouth come blessing and cursing. My brothers and sisters, this ought not to be so. 11 Does a spring pour forth from the same opening both fresh and brackish water? 12 Can a fig tree, my brothers and sisters, yield olives, or a grapevine figs? No more can salt water yield fresh.

## Supplementary Readings

### No Substitute for Obedience (Matthew 7:21–27)

21 Not everyone who says to me, "Lord, Lord," will enter the kingdom of heaven, but only the one who does the will of my Father in heaven. 22 On that day many will say to me, "Lord, Lord, did we not prophesy in your name, and cast out demons in your name, and do many deeds of power in your name?" 23 Then I will declare to them, "I never knew you; go away from me, you evildoers."

24 Everyone then who hears these words of mine and acts on them will be like a wise man who built his house on rock. 25 The rain fell, the floods came, and the winds blew and beat on that house, but it did not fall, because it had been founded on rock. 26 And everyone who hears these words of mine and does not act on them will be like a foolish man who built his house on sand. 27 The rain fell, and the floods came, and the winds blew and beat against that house, and it fell—and great was its fall!

*10 minutes*
*Choose questions according to your interest and time.*

**1** Based on James's statements so far in the letter, what kinds of action does James mean by "works"?

**2** How would you summarize the relationship between faith and action that James describes in this reading?

**3** What kinds of mistakes does James refer to in 3:2?

**4** What does James mean by "save" (2:14)? Refer to this week's reading and earlier readings.

**5** Does James say that we are saved by our actions rather than by our faith?

## A Guide to the Reading

*If participants have not read this section already, read it aloud. Otherwise go on to "Questions for Application."*

**2:14–19.** James continues to urge us to respond to the saving word of truth, implanted in us by God (1:18, 21). He has told us that hearing God's word without responding to it is not real hearing (1:22–27). Now he puts this idea in different terms: believing in God without acting on that belief is not real believing. The Greek word translated here as "works" means deeds, accomplishments. By "having works" James means putting into practice the commands of justice and mercy that lie at the heart of God's law.

James asks rhetorically whether faith can save us (2:14). More literally, he asks, "Can *that* faith save you?"—that is, faith without actions motivated by faith. He then goes on to show that faith minus actions is not faith at all. If actions are stripped away from faith, what remains is just a horrible mockery.

The speaker in the example *appears* to be a person of faith; he or she pronounces words of blessing: literally, "Go in peace, be warmed and filled!"—that is, be warmed and filled by God. Biblical scholar Sophie Laws remarks, "Confronted with a case of need, he commits it with prayer to God, who clothes the naked and feeds the hungry." But only an ignoramus ("you senseless person"—2:20) would think that our confidence in God is a *substitute* for efforts to provide what is needed. A poor person cannot wear or eat a blessing. This is faith without obedience to God, religion without commitment. With this truncated faith, a person goes piously to church but recognizes no obligation to the people with whom he or she worships. James denounces this kind of faith as corpselike (2:26). Why, even demons have this faith-without-deeds (2:19)! James is not setting faith and actions in opposition to each other; he is drawing a contrast between dead faith and living faith. As scholar Peter Davids observes, works are not an added extra to faith any more than breath is an added extra to a living body.

**2:20–26.** James calls faith without actions "barren." The Greek word means useless, unproductive, out of order, not in service. Faith without deeds is like an old dishwasher that has stopped working: in one sense it is still a dishwasher; in another sense it is just a piece of junk taking up space.

James points to Abraham as someone whose faith *was* completed in action. Abraham believed God's promise that he

**46**

would become the father of a great nation (Genesis 15:5–6); later he demonstrated his faith when God told him to sacrifice his only son (Genesis 22). By putting his faith into practice under this grievous test, Abraham was "justified," that is, he became a just and righteous person. His "faith was brought to completion": he became truly and wholeheartedly dedicated to God. By his obedience under trial, Abraham became a shining example to us of a person who becomes "mature and complete" by enduring hardships with faith (1:3–4). Thus Abraham became a "friend of God"—a person entirely committed to God's standards and instructions. He was no longer double-minded, torn between love for God and love for the world.

Both Abraham and Rahab (verses 21–25) were honored in Jewish tradition for showing unreserved hospitality to strangers—a fulfillment of the royal law of love of neighbor (Genesis 18:1–8; Joshua 2:1–21).

**3:1–4.** Earlier James declared that words are no substitute for action (2:14–17). Yet words are a *kind* of action. Our words have positive or negative effects on other people. This is the subject James now takes up. James views the mouth as a rudder for our whole being. If only we would take control of it, we could guide our whole self toward what is right and good.

**3:5–12.** A truly mature man or woman ("perfect"—3:2) would speak only what is constructive, useful, and true. Yet my arrogance, my pretensions to holiness, my desire to magnify myself at others' expense, my schemes to advance my own interests—all seep into my speech from morning to night. Through my speech I echo the distorted values of my society, thereby absorbing them into myself (3:6 could be translated, "the tongue is the world of wickedness established among our members; it pollutes the entire body"). My speech betrays my dividedness between love of God and love of self (3:9–12).

Yet St. Augustine pointed out that James "does not literally say *no one* can tame the tongue, but *no human being*. By the mercy of God, with the help of God, it can be mastered."

## Questions for Application

*40 minutes*
*Choose questions according to your interest and time.*

**1**  When has the example of someone's kindness or patience strengthened your faith in God? How might you imitate that person during this coming week?

**2**  In what situations today are Christians especially tempted to substitute lip service for action? Where do you face this temptation?

**3**  James suggests that control of the tongue is crucial for controlling our whole being. Why would this be the case?

**4** When have you seen words hurt or help? How has this affected how you speak to, and about, other people?

**5** About whom do you tend to speak uncharitably? What stops you from changing?

**6** In what ways are you a peacemaker or a peace destroyer in your family and parish? What fires do you fan or extinguish by the things you say?

**Listen carefully to one another's contributions and add to them. Be careful never to dominate the discussion.**

Oletta Wald, *The Joy of Discovery in Bible Study*

## Approach to Prayer

*15 minutes*
*Use this approach—or create your own!*

---

♦ Pray together these verses from Psalm 119. End with an Our Father.

Teach me, O LORD, the way of
    your statutes,
    and I will observe it to the end.
Give me understanding, that I
    may keep your law
    and observe it with my whole
    heart,
Lead me in the path of your
    commandments,
    for I delight in it.
Turn my heart to your decrees,
    and not to selfish gain.
Turn my eyes from looking at
    vanities;
    give me life in your ways. . . .

The LORD is my portion;
    I promise to keep your words.
I implore your favor with all my
    heart;
    be gracious to me according to
    your promise.
When I think of your ways,
    I turn my feet to your decrees;
I hurry and do not delay
    to keep your
    commandments. . . .
At midnight I rise to praise you,
    because of your righteous
    ordinances. . . .
The earth, O LORD, is full of
    your steadfast love;
    teach me your statutes.

## Saints in the Making

### *Isn't It Shocking?*

*This section is a supplement for individual reading.*

S igrid Undset, the Nobel prize–winning Norwegian novelist, once described a visit she and her aunt paid to her aunt's friend in the Danish countryside when Undset was a child. The friend was upset with one of her neighbors. It seems that a couple of days before, the friend had been picking raspberries in her garden when a man from a nearby farm rode by on his horse and paused to say that he was going to fetch a doctor for his housekeeper, who had been almost kicked to death by a cow. The friend, however, thought he said "Cohen," not "cow," the two words being almost identical in Danish. When the man rode off, the woman went to town and spread the news that Mr. Cohen, who happened to be the steward on the farm, had kicked the housekeeper so hard that a doctor had to be called. The following day, a furious Mr. Cohen appeared at the friend's house, threatening a lawsuit. Undset recalled the woman's astonishment. "Isn't it awful to think anyone could be so ill-natured as to go straight to the steward and tell him I'd been saying he'd kicked the housekeeper? . . . Isn't it shocking the way folks gossip about you?"

Undset wrote that this woman was like many people she knew who "like good Christians...strove to keep Our Lord's ten commandments, and it was not till they came to the eighth that they showed any sign of fatigue. But at the eighth they seemed unable to take any more fences on the road to heaven; they were apt to give themselves a long rest there."

Undset included herself among those who find the eighth commandment challenging ("You shall not bear false witness against your neighbor"—Exodus 20:16). Part of the solution, she thought, was to carefully read James's teaching about the tongue (3:1–12). In addition, she proposed the formation of a fellowship of recovering gossipers under St. James's patronage. Members of the proposed Society of St. James would daily pray Psalm 141:3–4: "Set a watch, O Lord, before my mouth: and a door round about my lips. Incline not my heart to evil words: to make excuses in sins" (Douay translation). This was to be followed by an Our Father, a Hail Mary, and the invocation "St. James, pray for us."

Would anyone like to call an organizational meeting?

# A CALL TO CONVERSION

## Questions to Begin

*15 minutes*
*Use a question or two to get warmed up for the reading.*

1  What ambition have you been able to fulfill? What ambition have you not been able to fulfill?

2  Name one thing that you hope to do during the coming year.

*5 minutes*
*Read the passage aloud. Let individuals take turns reading*
*paragraphs.*

## The Reading: James 3:13–4:16

### Two Ways Lie before You

13 Who is wise and understanding among you? Show by your good
life that your works are done with gentleness born of wisdom. 14 But
if you have bitter envy and selfish ambition in your hearts, do not be
boastful and false to the truth. 15 Such wisdom does not come down
from above, but is earthly, unspiritual, devilish. 16 For where there is
envy and selfish ambition, there will also be disorder and wickedness
of every kind. 17 But the wisdom from above is first pure, then
peaceable, gentle, willing to yield, full of mercy and good fruits,
without a trace of partiality or hypocrisy.18 And a harvest of
righteousness is sown in peace for those who make peace.

4:1 Those conflicts and disputes among you, where do they come
from? Do they not come from your cravings that are at war within
you? 2 You want something and do not have it; so you commit
murder. And you covet something and cannot obtain it; so you engage
in disputes and conflicts. You do not have, because you do not ask.
3 You ask and do not receive, because you ask wrongly, in order to
spend what you get on your pleasures. 4 Adulterers! Do you not know
that friendship with the world is enmity with God? Therefore
whoever wishes to be a friend of the world becomes an enemy of God.

### Repentance Is Possible!

5 Or do you suppose that it is for nothing that the scripture says,
"God yearns jealously for the spirit that he has made to dwell in us"?
6 But he gives all the more grace; therefore it says,
"God opposes the proud,
but gives grace to the humble."
7 Submit yourselves therefore to God. Resist the devil, and he will flee
from you. 8 Draw near to God, and he will draw near to you. Cleanse
your hands, you sinners, and purify your hearts, you double-minded.
9 Lament and mourn and weep. Let your laughter be turned into
mourning and your joy into dejection. 10 Humble yourselves before
the Lord, and he will exalt you.

### Example of Arrogance

11 Do not speak evil against one another, brothers and sisters. Whoever speaks evil against another or judges another, speaks evil against the law and judges the law; but if you judge the law, you are not a doer of the law but a judge. 12 There is one lawgiver and judge who is able to save and to destroy. So who, then, are you to judge your neighbor?

13 Come now, you who say, "Today or tomorrow we will go to such and such a town and spend a year there, doing business and making money." 14 Yet you do not even know what tomorrow will bring. What is your life? For you are a mist that appears for a little while and then vanishes. 15 Instead you ought to say, "If the Lord wishes, we will live and do this or that." 16 As it is, you boast in your arrogance; all such boasting is evil.


## Supplementary Readings

### Stop Being Worldly (Luke 22:24–27)

24 A dispute also arose among them as to which one of them was to be regarded as the greatest. 25 But he said to them, "The kings of the Gentiles lord it over them; and those in authority over them are called benefactors. 26 But not so with you; rather the greatest among you must become like the youngest, and the leader like one who serves. 27 For who is greater, the one who is at the table or the one who serves? Is it not the one at the table? But I am among you as one who serves."

### Let God Be the Judge (Matthew 7:1–5)

1 Do not judge, so that you may not be judged. 2 For with the judgment you make you will be judged, and the measure you give will be the measure you get. 3 Why do you see the speck in your neighbor's eye, but do not notice the log in your own eye? 4 Or how can you say to your neighbor, "Let me take the speck out of your eye," while the log is in your own eye? 5 You hypocrite, first take the log out of your own eye, and then you will see clearly to take the speck out of your neighbor's eye.

*10 minutes*
*Choose questions according to your interest and time.*

**1**   Why does James refer to "bitter envy and selfish ambition" (3:14) as "wisdom" (3:15)?

**2**   What kinds of behavior would illustrate the two types of wisdom that James speaks about in 3:13–17?

**3**   What does James mean by "the world" (4:4)? Consider the range of meaning in his previous uses of the word (1:27; 2:5; 3:6).

**4**   Why is it impossible to be friendly with both God and the world (4:4)?

**5**   How do James's remarks in 4:11–16 relate to what he wrote in 3:13–4:10?

## A Guide to the Reading

*If participants have not read this section already, read it aloud. Otherwise go on to "Questions for Application."*

**3:13–4:4.** James has raised the problem of our double-mindedness (1:8): we want God's wisdom, yet only halfheartedly (1:5–7); we hear God's word, yet do not respond to it (1:19–25); we have faith, but do not translate that faith into active love for those in need (chapter 2); we bless God while speaking uncharitably about other people (3:9–12). Now James brings this problem to a head. Look, James says, there are two irreconcilable ways of living, one based on love of God and neighbor, the other based on love of self. If you take the second route, your "selfish ambition"—your unscrupulous determination to gain your own ends—will inevitably produce conflict within you and with other people (3:15–16; 4:1–2). But the first route, which involves humble submission to God (3:13; "gentleness" also means humility), leads to peace (3:17–18).

Just as there is a demonic faith-without-actions (2:19), there is also a demonic wisdom—an earthbound cleverness about how to get ahead of other people and satisfy one's own cravings for power and recognition (3:14–16). By contrast, true wisdom is "full of mercy": it knows how to bring happiness to other people.

Earlier James declared that God will give eternal life to "those who love him" (1:12). Now he forces me to ask myself, *Do I love God?* Or am I, to use James's harsh term, an adulterer (4:4)? To love God *and* the world is not to love God (4:4). Am I serving on the boards of competing corporations? Am I a fake (3:14)? Have I embraced the heavenly wisdom that is "pure," the wisdom of being totally devoted to God's will? Am I guided in my decisions by the heavenly wisdom that is impartial (3:17), that is, not mixed, not divided, not wavering between two contradictory paths?

**4:5–10.** If James's call to repentance has gotten our attention, he has some practical recommendations for us.

Verse 5 is obscure. The "scripture" quoted does not come from the Bible; it may come from a religious document that no longer exists. Scholars are uncertain about how the quotation should be translated. It may be speaking about the contrary tendencies that struggle within the human spirit—yet another reference to our inner dividedness. But James proclaims the superior strength of God's grace. While selfish longings are deeply rooted in us, God empowers us to overcome them (4:6). God gives the gift that enables us to overcome our double-mindedness.

But we must make the effort to grasp God's helping hand. While God's grace is essential, only those who humble themselves will experience it. Thus James calls us to make a vigorous response to the implanted word of faith that is able to save us (1:21): to "submit," "draw near," "cleanse," and "purify." Knowing that repentance that is not heartfelt is unlikely to be lasting, James urges us to grieve over our double-minded condition. It is healthy to feel some sorrow over the harm our self-seeking has caused other people. "Blessed are those who mourn" (Matthew 5:4). The point is not that we should go around under a melancholy cloud of guilt but that we should allow ourselves to experience regret over our worldly values, for such an experience can play a part in freeing us from them (see "A Living Tradition," page 61).

**4:11–12.** Biblical scholar Luke Timothy Johnson explains that "slander serves the double function of lowering my neighbor and elevating me; it takes away status from another and gives it to me. It is the perfect example of life as competition. Slander is a form of arrogance that seeks to assert oneself by destroying another." The person who speaks maliciously about someone else "speaks evil against the law," because the law of God forbids us to speak evil against each other ("You shall not go around as a slanderer among your people"—Leviticus 19:16). Like showing partiality (2:1–13), speaking evil of other people is an offense against the royal law of love of neighbor.

**4:13–16.** James's listeners may be pious enough in church and at home, but apparently they shut God out of the business world. Their lives are divided into two compartments. In the religious compartment they talk about a God who is Lord of all. In the secular compartment they act as though God does not exist. In a final note, James urges us to rely on God to plan our days. Planning is fine, provided it follows the model of one first-century traveling businessman, a tentmaker from Tarsus: "I will come to you soon, if the Lord wills" (St. Paul, 1 Corinthians 4:19).

## Questions for Application

*40 minutes*
*Choose questions according to your interest and time.*

---

**1**  In what ways are the earthbound attitudes described in 3:14–16 accepted and even promoted in society today? What words and expressions are sometimes used to give these attitudes the appearance of being harmless, healthy, even necessary?

---

**2**  Where can one find examples of people living according to the heavenly wisdom that James speaks about in 3:13, 17–18?

---

**3**  Recall a truly wise person whom you have known. What lasting impact has this person had on you? In what way do you imitate him or her?

**4** What does James's call to conversion (4:7–10) mean to you? What should you do to respond?

**5** Recount an incident in a novel or movie or play in which someone passed up the opportunity to repent. What was the result?

**We learn what the Bible means as we relate it to our life.**

Steve Mueller, *The Seeker's Guide to Reading the Bible*

## Approach to Prayer

*15 minutes*
*Use this approach—or create your own!*

---

◆ Pray an Our Father, then pray this portion of St. Francis of Assisi's prayer inspired by the Our Father.

"Your kingdom come,"
so that you may rule in us by
   your grace
and enable us to arrive at your
   kingdom,
where there is clear vision of you,
   perfect love for you,
   joyful union with you,
   everlasting delight in you.

"Your will be done on earth as it
   is in heaven,"
so that we may love you with all
   our heart,
   always thinking of you,
   with our whole soul always
      desiring you,
   with our whole mind directing
      all our attention to you,
   in everything, seeking your
      glory,
   and with our whole strength
      spending all our vigor and
      capacities only in obedience
      to your love.

## A Living Tradition

### *Cleansing Tears*

*This section is a supplement for individual reading.*

James tells us to "lament and mourn and weep" as we turn to God in repentance (4:9). Many spiritual writers have explored the constructive role of sorrow in the process of repentance. One such author was St. Robert Bellarmine (1542–1621), a Catholic theologian who composed a short book on the subject entitled *The Sighing of the Dove, Or the Value of Tears.* Here are a few of his thoughts.

**Reasons to weep over our sins.** The first source of tears is the consideration of the ugliness of sin. . . .

Our sin not only offends God; it harms other people, for by its example our sin invites them to evil. Thus it deflects them from their true end, which is God, and turns them toward an end that is contrary to God. . . .

A comparison of humanity with God is sufficient to bring forth a river of tears from the hardest human heart. . . . What is God, and what are we? God is the most loving and kindest Father, who if he should remove from us that which he could, we would be brought entirely to nothing. And can it be that of such a good father would be found such an evil child?

**The effects of sorrow over our sins.** Tears of repentance produce the hope of certain forgiveness and reconciliation with God, from which arises in the spirit of the penitent incomparable rejoicing. . . .

This is the power of holy tears flowing from true contrition of heart: it makes clear and calm the hearts of sinners after long dread and fear, just as after the darkness of dense storm clouds a heavy rainfall leaves the air clear and bright. The cause of this effect seems to be that through our sorrow the Holy Spirit gives testimony to our spirit that we are children of God (Romans 8:16), since our sins have become displeasing to us. The peace of God now exults in our hearts, and it is very plain to us that we are accepted by the Father with a kiss of heavenly peace, and a fine stole, and a ring of complete reconciliation (see Luke 15:22). . . .

The one who has tears as partner in prayer may rejoice, because after prayer he or she will go away without anxiety.

# Keep On Keeping On

## Questions to Begin

*15 minutes*
*Use a question or two to get warmed up for the reading.*

**1**  What do you often do when you're happy that you rarely do when you're unhappy?

**2**  Describe a helpful correction that you received from another person.

*5 minutes*
*Read the passage aloud. Let individuals take turns reading paragraphs.*

## The Reading: James 4:17–5:20

### Unshared Wealth

17 Anyone . . . who knows the right thing to do and fails to do it, commits sin.

5:1 Come now, you rich people, weep and wail for the miseries that are coming to you. 2 Your riches have rotted, and your clothes are moth-eaten. 3 Your gold and silver have rusted, and their rust will be evidence against you, and it will eat your flesh like fire. You have laid up treasure for the last days. 4 Listen! The wages of the laborers who mowed your fields, which you kept back by fraud, cry out, and the cries of the harvesters have reached the ears of the Lord of hosts. 5 You have lived on the earth in luxury and in pleasure; you have fattened your hearts in a day of slaughter. 6 You have condemned and murdered the righteous one, who does not resist you.

### Never Give Up

7 Be patient, therefore, beloved, until the coming of the Lord. The farmer waits for the precious crop from the earth, being patient with it until it receives the early and the late rains. 8 You also must be patient. Strengthen your hearts, for the coming of the Lord is near. 9 Beloved, do not grumble against one another, so that you may not be judged. See, the Judge is standing at the doors! 10 As an example of suffering and patience, beloved, take the prophets who spoke in the name of the Lord. 11 Indeed we call blessed those who showed endurance. You have heard of the endurance of Job, and you have seen the purpose of the Lord, how the Lord is compassionate and merciful.

12 Above all, my beloved, do not swear, either by heaven or by earth or by any other oath, but let your "Yes" be yes and your "No" be no, so that you may not fall under condemnation.

### Prayer, Healing, and Forgiveness

13 Are any among you suffering? They should pray. Are any cheerful? They should sing songs of praise. 14 Are any among you sick? They should call for the elders of the church and have them pray over them, anointing them with oil in the name of the Lord. 15 The prayer

of faith will save the sick, and the Lord will raise them up; and anyone who has committed sins will be forgiven. 16 Therefore confess your sins to one another, and pray for one another, so that you may be healed. The prayer of the righteous is powerful and effective. 17 Elijah was a human being like us, and he prayed fervently that it might not rain, and for three years and six months it did not rain on the earth. 18 Then he prayed again, and the heaven gave rain and the earth yielded its harvest.

19 My brothers and sisters, if anyone among you wanders from the truth and is brought back by another, 20 you should know that whoever brings back a sinner from wandering will save the sinner's soul from death and will cover a multitude of sins.


## Supplementary Readings

See That Your Neighbor Has Bread *Today* (Proverbs 3:27–28)

27 Do not withhold good from those to whom it is due,
    when it is in your power to do it.
28 Do not say to your neighbor, "Go, and come again,
    tomorrow I will give it"—when you have it with you.

Don't Make the Needy Wait for Help (Sirach 29:8–12)

8 Be patient with someone in humble circumstances,
    and do not keep him waiting for your alms.
9 Help the poor for the commandment's sake,
    and in their need do not send them away empty-handed.
10 Lose your silver for the sake of a brother or a friend,
    and do not let it rust under a stone and be lost.
11 Lay up your treasure according to the commandments of
    the Most High,
    and it will profit you more than gold.
12 Store up almsgiving in your treasury,
    and it will rescue you from every disaster.

*10 minutes*
*Choose questions according to your interest and time.*

**1**   Does James condemn the mere possession of wealth? Consider earlier statements in the letter as well as this week's reading.

**2**   What problems does James associate with wealth?

**3**   Only a minority of people in society today make a living by farming. What modern situations could provide images that would make the same point as James's agricultural images in 5:7?

**4**   What impression of James's character and personality have you formed from reading his letter? To whom would you compare him?

**5**   Compare James's remark on prayer in 5:17 with what he says about prayer in 1:5–8 and 4:2–4. How would you summarize James's teaching about petitioning God?

## A Guide to the Reading

*If participants have not read this section already, read it aloud. Otherwise go on to "Questions for Application."*

**5:1–6.** James directs a stern warning to the wealthy. Their wealth stands as a double accusation against them, he declares, for it should have been used to alleviate the suffering of the needy (5:2–3) and it has come to them through fraud (5:4). Too bad they have not used their resources for others rather than for themselves (Sirach 29:8–12; see page 72).

In the view of the New Testament writers, Jesus' death and resurrection have brought the human race into its final period of interaction with God, sometimes called the "last days" (Acts 2:17; 2 Timothy 3:1; Hebrews 1:2). Thus James tells the rich literally, "You have laid up treasure *in* the last days" (5:3; italics mine). They are not synchronized with God's activity. God's kingdom is already arriving, and God is inviting us to devote ourselves fully to his project of cultivating mercy in the world. But even at this late date, the wealthy are still focused on improving their earthly situation.

James tells the wealthy, "You have fattened your hearts" (5:5). By faring sumptuously every day while other people are hungry (compare Luke 16:19–31), the wealthy have hardened their consciences against their neighbors' suffering (see Isaiah 6:10 as quoted in Matthew 13:15). The issue is not whether we like to eat well but whether we are concerned about our neighbors who do not have enough to eat. I am not wealthy, but I know that I too am addressed by James's words.

**5:7–11.** Apparently most of James's readers were poor (see 2:5–7). Some of them may have been victims of the exploitation that James just referred to (5:4–6), and there may have been political unrest in the face of this injustice. James does not take injustice lightly (as 5:1–6 make clear). Nevertheless, he tells his readers to leave the judgment of persons to God (5:9). James urges us to trust in God and to take a forbearing, patient approach to anyone who has hurt us (5:7–9). God is "compassionate and merciful" (verse 11); let us imitate him. Of course, James does not discourage us from taking vigorous peaceful measures to correct injustice, especially injustices suffered by other people.

Pointing to the patient endurance of Old Testament prophets, James focuses not on their deaths but on the fact that they "spoke" (5:10). Luke Timothy Johnson observes that "this suggests that he is thinking of the whole course of the prophetic mission, with its continual difficulties, struggles against opposition and rejection, and . . . temptations to despair. . . . It is in the course of their lives, rather than in their deaths, that the prophets serve as an example of patience."

**5:12.** In formal situations, such as when testifying in court, the taking of an oath expresses a commitment to telling the truth. In everyday life, however, taking oaths serves as yet another example of double-mindedness. If I constantly use oaths to give credibility to my words, people will suspect that I am not telling the truth when I do not use an oath. A related problem may also arise: the more often I swear, the more likely it is that I will eventually fall into perjury.

**5:13–20.** After so much discussion of harmful speech, it seems appropriate for James to end with a few words about the good we can do with our words. James recommends that we saturate our lives with an awareness of God by singing and praying (5:13). Verses 14 and 15 envision a community in which the sick people are not isolated but feel free to call on the leaders to pray for and visit them (see "A Living Tradition," page 71). Presumably James intends for us to pray both for physical healing and for wisdom and patience to endure suffering (see 1:2–4; 5:10).

James has said that we cannot expect God to answer our prayers if we do not pray with a sincere desire for God's will (1:6; 4:3). Now he says that God does respond to the prayer of those committed to following God's ways (5:16). "The Lord will raise them up"—perhaps from sickness, certainly in the resurrection.

We may let Bede have the last word, with his comment on the last verse: "It must not be overlooked that this turning back of someone who strays is accomplished not only by speaking but very often also by acting well. For if anyone shows his neighbors the examples of good action and turns them back to imitating the works of almsgiving or hospitality or of the other virtues which they had neglected, even though his tongue be silent, he actually executes the office of teaching and obtains from the judge a sure reward in return for the salvation of his brother or sister whom he has corrected."

## Questions for Application

*40 minutes*
*Choose questions according to your interest and time.*

**1** How much of our personal futures can we control? What is beyond our control? How much do you trust God with your future? How can a person measure his or her trust in God?

**2** Who do you know that is in ill health and would welcome a visit, a note, a phone call? What will you do?

**3** What "silver" of yours (5:3) is corroding while others are hungry? What could you do to help meet their need?

**4** James cites Job and Elijah as examples of patience and prayer. Who in your life exemplifies James's teaching? What can you learn from them?

**5** Describe a situation in which you let an opportunity to do good slip away. What did you learn from this experience?

**6** Regarding 5:13–15, biblical scholar Pheme Perkins writes: "One of the most important effects of healing services that involve the whole community, not just the sick, is breaking the barriers of silence and isolation that illness often imposes on the sick and their families. Members of the congregation feel free to ask people how they are doing, to send cards, or to drop in for a visit even if the person is not a personal friend." How successful is your parish in drawing sick members into its community life? How could you help your parish move in this direction?

**The Bible was not given to us merely to satisfy our curiosity, but to change and redirect our lives. God gave us his word to reveal himself to us, and to evoke a response from us according to what is revealed.**

*How to Lead Small Group Bible Studies*

## Approach to Prayer

*15 minutes*
*Use this approach—or create your own!*

♦ Take a few minutes to mention people who are sick or are experiencing other difficulties. Then pray Psalm 13 for them, given below. End with an Our Father.

How long, O LORD? Will you
forget me forever?
How long will you hide your
face from me?
How long must I bear pain in my
soul,
and have sorrow in my heart
all day long?
How long shall my enemy be
exalted over me?

Consider and answer me, O
LORD my God!
Give light to my eyes, or I will
sleep the sleep of death,
and my enemy will say, "I have
prevailed";
my foes will rejoice because I
am shaken.
But I trusted in your steadfast
love;
my heart shall rejoice in your
salvation.
I will sing to the LORD,
because he has dealt
bountifully with me.

# A Living Tradition

## The Anointing of the Sick

*This section is a supplement for individual reading.*

James urges us not only to endure suffering with faith but also to ask God to free us from suffering. "Are any among you sick? They should call for the elders of the church and have them pray over them, anointing them with oil in the name of the Lord. The prayer of faith will save the sick, and the Lord will raise them up; and anyone who has committed sins will be forgiven" (5:14–15).

James's words are evidence that the early Church carried on the tradition of praying for healing that began with Jesus. Healing was a prominent part of Jesus' ministry and a sign of God's approaching kingdom. Jesus commissioned his apostles to continue this aspect of his work. Mark tells us that Jesus sent them out two by two to preach and to heal. "So they went out and proclaimed that all should repent. They cast out many demons, and anointed with oil many who were sick and cured them" (Mark 6:12–13). After Jesus' resurrection, the apostles handed on this tradition of praying for healing to the next generation of Christians.

Through the centuries, the Church has continued to practice this expression of Jesus' "preferential love for the sick," as the *Catechism of the Catholic Church* puts it (section 1503). Indeed, the Church regards prayer with anointing as one of the seven sacraments through which Christ makes himself present to us and acts in our lives. The sacrament is called the anointing of the sick. In the words of the sixteenth-century Council of Trent, "This sacred anointing of the sick was instituted by Christ our Lord as a true and proper sacrament of the New Testament. It is alluded to indeed by Mark, but is recommended to the faithful and promulgated by James the apostle and brother of the Lord."

The sacrament is designed for everyone whose life is endangered by serious illness or the frailty of old age. Through it, God renews faith and brings forgiveness of sins through the grace of the Spirit and draws those who are sick into union with Jesus in his suffering on our behalf. At times, God also restores the physical health of the person who receives the sacrament.

For a brief, informative discussion of the sacrament of the anointing of the sick, see the *Catechism of the Catholic Church,* sections 1499–1532.

## Goods Are Meant for Everyone

### *James Urges Us to Share with Those in Need*

In chapter 5, James directs a warning to wealthy people: "Come now, you rich people." Most of us do not think of ourselves as rich. But many of us who are using this booklet are well-off compared to very many people around the world who suffer hunger, sickness, and degradation because their material resources are so inadequate. We "relatively rich" people may find something in James's words that speaks to us.

To the wealthy of his own day, James had this to say: "Weep and wail for the miseries that are coming to you. Your riches have rotted, and your clothes are moth-eaten. Your gold and silver have rusted, and their rust will be evidence against you. . . . Listen! The wages of the laborers who mowed your fields, which you kept back by fraud, cry out, and the cries of the harvesters have reached the ears of the Lord of hosts" (5:1–4).

James brings a double accusation against rich people. They use their wealth to support a luxurious lifestyle rather than sharing it with the needy, and they fail to pay their laborers the agreed-on wages. It is easy to see what is wrong with holding back wages. But James seems to regard it as equally wrong for the wealthy to enjoy the pleasures and prestige their wealth makes possible. Why?

The answer lies partly in the economic limitations of his society. Before the industrial revolution in the eighteenth century, no economy could achieve sustained, long-term growth. Locked into a peasant agricultural framework, and with only very gradual technological change, the economies of the past reached a growth ceiling. Their capacity to produce goods and services simply maxed out. Constant innovation makes it possible for modern economies to grow indefinitely, and though the growth brings great wealth only to a few, it also benefits many other members of society. This kind of general advancement was impossible in pre-industrial societies. The economic pie could not be enlarged, and so one person could get a larger slice only by shrinking someone else's portion. If a few people were getting rich, many others were necessarily being impoverished. Thus in James's time the mere possession of wealth was evidence that someone had oppressed or defrauded someone else.

The fact that modern economies tend to improve the lot of most members of society does not, however, mean that we are free to lavish on ourselves whatever wealth we acquire. For even if our affluence has not been achieved by our exploiting other people, we possess it in a world where large numbers of people do not have the basic necessities. In this situation, a principle comes into play that was implicit in James's warning to the wealthy but has become explicit in the Christian tradition. This is the principle that God has given the earth to the human race for the good of the human race. Thus the material resources that we accumulate should ultimately serve the needs of the whole human family. James took the wealthy to task for violating this principle. The expensive clothes hanging unused in their closets (5:2) symbolized their surplus, which they were failing to make available to their desperately needy neighbors.

In the Catholic tradition, this principle has been called the "universal destination of earthly goods." The bishops at Vatican Council II (1962–65) explained it by saying that "God destined the earth and all it contains for all human beings and all peoples so that all created things would be shared fairly by all under the guidance of justice tempered by charity." Consequently, the bishops said, each of us should regard our possessions not as exclusively our own but as common to others, in the sense of being intended to benefit others as well (*Pastoral Constitution on the Church in the Modern World,* section 69). John Paul II has said that in the economic sphere, the universal destination of earthly goods is "the fundamental principle of the moral order."

Does this mean that the Catholic Church opposes private property? Far from it. The Catholic tradition has viewed private property as an irreplaceable element of a just society. Private property is the mechanism by which many of the world's material goods are best developed and conserved. But since God has given the earth to the whole human race, each of us possesses our property in trust for the common good. God puts resources in our individual control so that we might use them for the benefit of all, especially for those who are in serious need. Pius XI declared, "The right to own private property has been given to man by nature, or rather by the creator himself, not only in order that individuals may be able to provide for their own needs and those of their families, but also that by means of it, the goods which the creator has destined for the human race may truly serve this purpose" (*Quadragesimo Anno,* section 45).

Beginning in the New Testament and proceeding through Christian writings of the first centuries, we find abundant testimony to the seriousness with which Christians have taken this principle. To cite just one example, Aristides, a second-century Greek Christian, wrote of his fellow Christians: "They love one another and do not overlook the widow and deliver the orphan from him who treats him harshly. He who has supplies the needs of him who has not, without grudging. And if there is among them any that is poor and needy, and if they have no spare food, they fast two or three days to supply the needy with what they need." Now *that* is truly putting into practice the principle of the universal destination of earthly goods!

In James's day, with its limited opportunities for economic development, people with surplus wealth had limited ways in which they could fulfill the social obligation their wealth placed on them. The simple, straightforward giving of money or goods was the main option for sharing wealth with the needy (see Acts 2:45; 4:32–37). By contrast, in our more varied and dynamic economy, we have a wider range of opportunities for useful sharing of resources. Catholic legal philosopher John Finnis points out that besides simply giving away our money we can invest in the production of useful goods, provide jobs by developing businesses, offer loans to nonprofit institutions, contribute our time and talents to charitable organizations, and share our skills and know-how with those eager to learn.

The conviction that the needy people around us have a claim on our resources is deeply rooted in the Christian tradition. From the earliest Christian centuries we see it expressed by one teacher after another. Yet the principle has never been an easy one to put into practice. In the seventeenth century, noted Italian theologian Robert Bellarmine collected statements of respected Christian teachers from the second century to his own day that all pointed to the conviction that surplus wealth justly belongs to those who need it. His book almost never made it to the printer, because the church official who had to approve its publication objected that Bellarmine was introducing a strange, new teaching! Bellarmine's book was published only when Pope Pius V overruled this obviously false objection.

Along with the principle of the universal destination of the earth's goods goes the principle that each of us must decide what our needs are, what surplus is for us, and how we might best direct our surplus to the common good. St. Paul exemplified this principle of individual responsibility when he was collecting charitable contributions from the Christians in Corinth: "I do not say this as a command, but I am testing the genuineness of your love. . . . For you know the generous act of our Lord Jesus Christ, that though he was rich, yet for your sakes he became poor, so that by his poverty you might become rich" (2 Corinthians 8:8–9). He added, "Each of you must give as you have made up your mind, not reluctantly or under compulsion, for God loves a cheerful giver" (2 Corinthians 9:7).

In the second century, a Palestinian Christian named Justin (often referred to as Justin Martyr) wrote that when contributions were collected for the poor after worship on Sunday, "they who are well-to-do and willing give what each thinks fit." In the same century, the African Christian Tertullian likewise emphasized the voluntary nature of Christian giving: "On the monthly day, if he likes, each puts in a small donation, but only if it be his pleasure, and only if he be able, for there is no compulsion, all is voluntary. These gifts are . . . taken . . . to support and bury poor people, to supply the wants of boys and girls destitute of means and parents, and of old persons confined now to the house."

So we are addressed by James and by the Christian tradition after him. "Goods are meant for everyone," John Paul II has said. Each of us must decide how we will respond. In making our response, we may be helped by a statement that the American bishops made in their pastoral letter on the American economy in 1986: "Compassion is the bridge between mere seeing to action" (*Economic Justice for All*, section 43). They were speaking about the Samaritan in Jesus' parable (Luke 10:25–37). He saw a man in need and felt compassion, and so he acted. As Jesus said, "Go and do likewise."

## Suggestions for Bible Discussion Groups

Like a camping trip, a Bible discussion group works best if you agree on where you're going and how you intend to get there. Many groups use their first meeting to talk over such questions and reach a consensus. Here is a checklist of issues, with bits of advice from people who have experience in Bible discussions. (A planning discussion will go more smoothly if the leaders have thought through the following issues beforehand.)

**Agree on your purpose.** Are you getting together to gain wisdom and direction for your lives? to finally get acquainted with the Bible? to support one another in following Christ? to encourage those who are exploring—or reexploring—the Church? for other reasons?

**Agree on attitudes.** For example: "We're all beginners here." "We're here to help each other understand and respond to God's word." "We're not here to offer counseling or direction to each other." "We want to read Scripture prayerfully." What do *you* wish to emphasize? Make it explicit!

**Agree on ground rules.** Barbara J. Fleischer, in her useful book *Facilitating for Growth,* recommends that a group clearly state its approach to the following:

- *Preparation.* Do we agree to read the material and prepare the answers to the questions before each meeting?
- *Attendance.* What kind of priority will we give to our meetings?
- *Self-revelation.* Are we willing to help the others in the group gradually get to know us—our weaknesses as well as our strengths, our needs as well as our gifts?
- *Listening.* Will we commit ourselves to listening to each other?
- *Confidentiality.* Will we keep everything that is shared *with* the group *in* the group?
- *Discretion.* Will we refrain from sharing about the faults and sins of people outside the group?
- *Encouragement and support.* Will we give as well as receive?
- *Participation.* Will we give each person time and opportunity to make a contribution?

You could probably take a pen and draw a circle around *listening* and *confidentiality*. Those two points are especially important.

The following items could be added to Fleischer's list:

◆ *Relationship with parish.* Is our group part of the adult faith-formation program? independent but operating with the express approval of the pastor? not a parish-based group?

◆ *New members.* Will we let new members join us once we have begun the six weeks of discussions?

### Agree on housekeeping.

◆ *When will we meet?*

◆ *How often will we meet?* Meeting weekly or every other week is best if you can manage it. William Riley remarks, "Meetings once a month are too distant from each other for the threads of the last session not to be lost" *(The Bible Study Group: An Owner's Manual).*

◆ *How long will meetings run?*

◆ *Where will we meet?*

◆ *Is any setup needed?* Christine Dodd writes that "the problem with meeting in a place like a church hall is that it can be very soul-destroying" given the cold, impersonal feel of many church facilities. If you have to meet in a church facility, Dodd recommends doing something to make the area homey *(Making Scripture Work).*

◆ *Who will host the meetings?* Leaders and hosts are not necessarily the same people.

◆ *Will we have refreshments?* Who will provide them?

◆ *What about child care?* Most experienced leaders of Bible discussion groups discourage bringing infants or other children to adult Bible discussions.

**Agree on leadership.** You need someone to facilitate—to keep the discussion on track, to see that everyone has a chance to speak, to help the group stay on schedule. Rena Duff, editor of the newsletter *Sharing God's Word Today,* recommends having two or three people take turns leading the discussions.

It's okay if the leader is not an expert on the Bible. You have this booklet, and if questions come up that no one can answer, you can delegate a participant to do a little research between meetings. It's important for the leader to set an example of listening, to draw out the quieter members (and occasionally restrain the more vocal ones), to move the group on when it gets stuck, to remind the members of their agreements, and to summarize what the group is accomplishing.

Bible discussion is an opportunity to experience the fulfillment of Jesus' promise "Where two or three are gathered in my name, I am there among them" (Matthew 18:20). Put your discussion group in Jesus' hands. Pray for the guidance of the Spirit. And have a great time exploring God's word together!

## Suggestions for Individuals

Y ou can use this booklet just as well for individual study as for group discussion. While discussing the Bible with other people can be a rich experience, there are advantages to reading on your own. For example:

◆ You can focus on the points that interest you most.

◆ You can go at your own pace.

◆ You can be completely relaxed and unashamedly honest in your answers to all the questions, since you don't have to share them with anyone!

My suggestions for using this booklet on your own are these:

◆ Don't skip "Questions to Begin." The questions can help you as an individual reader warm up to the topic of the reading.

◆ Take your time on "Questions for Careful Reading" and "Questions for Application." While a group will probably not have enough time to work on all the questions, you can allow yourself the time to consider all of them if you are using the booklet by yourself.

◆ After reading the "Guide to the Reading," go back and reread the Scripture text before answering the questions for application.

◆ Take the time to look up all the parenthetical Scripture references.

◆ Since you control the pace, give yourself plenty of opportunities to reflect on the meaning of the letter of James for you. Let your reading be an opportunity for these words to become God's words to you.

**Resources**

## Bibles

The following editions of the Bible contain the full set of biblical books recognized by the Catholic Church, along with a great deal of useful explanatory material:

- The Catholic Study Bible (Oxford University Press), which uses the text of the New American Bible
- The Catholic Bible: Personal Study Edition (Oxford University Press), which also uses the text of the New American Bible
- The New Jerusalem Bible, the regular (not the reader's) edition (Doubleday)

## Books

- Raymond E. Brown, *An Introduction to the New Testament,* The Anchor Bible Reference Library (New York: Doubleday, 1997), 725–47.
- Luke Timothy Johnson, *The Letter of James: A New Translation with Introduction and Commentary,* The Anchor Bible, vol. 37A (New York: Doubleday, 1995).
- Luke Timothy Johnson, *The Writings of the New Testament: An Interpretation,* revised edition (Minneapolis: Fortress Press, 1999), 507–20.
- Sophie Laws, *The Epistle of James,* Black's New Testament Commentaries, vol. 16 (Peabody, Mass.: Hendrickson Publishers, 1993).
- Pheme Perkins, *First and Second Peter, James, and Jude,* Interpretation, a Bible Commentary for Teaching and Preaching (Louisville, Ky.: John Knox Press, 1995), 83–140.

How has Scripture had an impact on your life? Was this booklet helpful to you in your study of the Bible? Please send comments, suggestions, and personal experiences to Kevin Perrotta, c/o Trade Editorial Department, Loyola Press, 3441 N. Ashland Ave., Chicago, IL 60657.